Schwerpunktthema

Abitur Englisch

Outsourced

A Film Study

W0277495

Cornelsen

Outsourced A Film Study

von Christina Diehr und Cordula Rohlmann-Reineke

Verlagsredaktion
Ingrid von der Felsen-Ferguson; Katrin Heinecke

Layout und technische Umsetzung
Annika Preyhs für Buchgestaltung+, Berlin

Umschlaggestaltung
hawemannundmosch, Konzeption und Gestaltung, Berlin

www.cornelsen.de

1. Auflage, 2. Druck 2013

Alle Drucke dieser Auflage sind inhaltlich unverändert und können im Unterricht nebeneinander verwendet werden.

Druck: H. Heenemann, Berlin

ISBN 978-3-06-033149-9

Inhalt gedruckt auf säurefreiem Papier aus nachhaltiger Forstwirtschaft.

POST-VIEWING ACTIVITIES

Dear student,

We are living in a globalized world where modern technology dissolves geographical borders and people have to be increasingly flexible in order to keep up with the pace of economic change. Outsourcing is an aspect of globalization which affects many people, e.g. those whose work has been shifted from their native country to a foreign land or those who have to put up with working and living conditions very different from what they have been used to previously.

In these transient times cultural traditions may offer stability; however, they may also lead to misunderstandings and problems when people from different cultural backgrounds have to work together.

Cultural differences do not, of course, only pose difficulties, they can also enrich people's lives. Seeing one's country from the outside can provide valuable insights into one's own behaviour and attitudes. Experiencing another culture inevitably helps to improve one's ability to adjust to new value systems and thus reassess previously held opinions and views. This process ideally works in both directions.

Outsourced manages to enlighten its viewers on such a complex economic and socio-cultural topic in a thoroughly entertaining way.

We have structured this booklet in such a way that you will be able to work on the film and its manifold aspects on your own.

After reading the plot and scene index, you might consider some questions on the film to get you thinking about the topics and to help you plan how to deal with the film.

The pre-viewing activities are designed to help you get into the work by concentrating more specifically on outsourcing and India.

The while-viewing tasks will give you guidance on how to analyse the ways in which the main topics of the film are presented. The cultural clash between Todd and the Indian call centre agents plays a central role here. More detailed information about film-making can be found at the back of this booklet, and if you would like to explore the matter further, you would be well advised to consult the additional material presented in the CD-ROM *At the Cutting Edge* (see inside front cover).

Finally, a selection of post-viewing tasks will offer you increased insight into further implications of the overarching issue of globalization/ outsourcing.

You will also find various assignments designed along the lines of the 'Operatoren der Zentralen Prüfungen' that you already know from your English lessons. We have taken special care to ensure that you get practice in each of the relevant fields from comprehension, analysis and comment right through to creative writing.

Enjoy both the film itself and (with a bit of luck) your work on it!

Christina Diehr *Cordula Rohlmann-Reineke*

OUTSOURCED (2006)

Directed by	John Jeffcoat	**Starring**	Josh Hamilton
Writing credits	George Wing		Ayesha Dharker
	John Jeffcoat		Asif Basra
Produced by	Tom Gorai		

THE PLOT

In order to cut costs, call centre manager Todd Anderson's job and the jobs of his department are outsourced from Seattle to a small city in India. Anderson is sent to India to train his Indian replacement Puro for his new role selling typical American kitsch via India. It is Todd's only chance to keep his job, so he reluctantly travels to India.

On his way to Gharapuri Todd experiences a completely new and unfamiliar world. Arriving in the newly-established call centre, a small shabby building, Todd notices that the employees are unable to fulfil the strict American requirement of selling the company's products within six minutes per call. Anderson has to coach them intensively to reduce their sales time from 15 minutes to six.

At first Todd tries to encourage the call centre's employees to adopt the American way of working, advising the Indians to pretend to be American. This attempt turns out to be a complete failure.

Todd realizes that Asha is the only member of the team who is able to meet his expectations and to lead the team successfully. She is also the one to make him realize that he has a lot to learn too, about India – and about himself. Thus he slowly becomes more receptive to the Indian way of life and starts really appreciating his stay in India.

During a business trip – and after the apparent intervention by Kali, the goddess of destruction and renewal – Todd and Asha end up in the Kama Sutra suite of a luxury hotel. They spend an intimate night together but are aware of the fact that their relationship has no future. Asha is engaged to a man she was promised to at the age of four. Todd can't understand her wanting to marry this man but she is sure she can learn to love him – like her parents once did after their marriage.

Shortly after reducing the sales time to six minutes per call, Todd's boss Dave from Seattle appears in India to inform Todd that his department is going to be outsourced once again. This time it is to China, since it is even cheaper to operate from there. Todd is to be sent to Shanghai to start all over again, but refuses do so, returning instead to Seattle. Puro, his former Indian trainee, proves a willing candidate to take the job in China.

Back in his apartment in Seattle, Todd receives a call from Asha.

SCENE INDEX

Chapter	Time	Characters / Action
	0:00:00 – 0:00:45	**Opening credits**
1	0:00:46 – 0:03:47	
		Todd – working in a call centre – is summoned by his boss Dave into his office. Dave informs him that the company is moving the call centre to India. Todd will have to train the Indian office manager how to work efficiently. Todd can only come home when the MPI (minutes per incident) is under 6 minutes. If he does not agree to the terms he will lose his job and benefits – just like his colleagues.
2	0:03:48 – 0:11:13	**Welcome to Bombay**
		As Todd fails to notice the sign reading 'Mr Toad' upon his arrival at Mumbai airport where he is supposed to be picked up, he tries to find his own way to Gharapuri. Todd manages to jump on a crowded train and finally arrives in Gharapuri, where he first buys some gola (Indian water ice) as he is very thirsty. Todd is welcomed by Purohit Narsimacharya Virajnariandu (Puro), the Indian office manager he has been sent to train.
3	0:11:14 – 0:18:46	**You like India?**
		On their way to Puro's aunt's house he and Todd get to know each other a little. Todd gets an impression of Gharapuri, which is smaller but also dirtier and more crowded than what he has seen of Mumbai. Upon arriving at Aunt Ji's, Todd gets his first lessons on some basics of Indian culture. In his room Todd's attention is caught by the picture of a goddess holding the cut-off head of a man in her hands. Later when walking around the beautiful walled garden, Todd peeks over the wall and sees a different world: crowds of laundry workers and their poor housing.
4	0:18:47 – 0:22:41	**The Gola!**
		Because of the time difference between India and the USA the call centre only operates at night. On their way to work Puro tells Todd that with his new job he will be able to get married. Todd discovers that the centre is up and running – but the building has not been finished yet. Todd meets the Indian call centre agents. When Todd feels the first signs of diarrhoea he hurries home. On his way a little boy begs for some money and steals Todd's mobile. At home Todd is confronted with a traditional Indian toilet.
5	0:22:42 – 0:29:30	**Rubber**
		Back at the call centre Todd sets up a training session on 'American culture' in order to improve customer satisfaction. For Todd the Indian accent is a key issue he wants to work on: The Indian call centre agents are to behave as though they were Americans in the USA. Todd goes on to explain the products the call centre agents have to sell.

Chapter	Time	Characters / Action
6	0:29:31 – 0:37:01	**Cheeseburger**
		Todd intensifies the training on cultural differences, especially on the choice of words (e.g. rubber vs. eraser). Having learned that his former girlfriend has a new boyfriend, Todd feels very lonely, but when he sees an ad for MacDonnells he takes a taxi to Mumbai to eat a cheeseburger. In Mumbai Todd discovers that MacDonnell's is not McDonald's. Another expat tells him all about the extent of outsourcing in India.
7	0:37:02 – 0:46:49	**Holi**
		As he is leaving for work Todd overlooks a note warning him not to leave the house. Outside he sees men with coloured powder all over them. The empty streets are also full of this powder. Puro tries to protect Todd from it, but both of them are hit by the powder. It is the festival of Holi. Finally Todd participates in the fun himself. After a dip in a public pool Todd is having something to eat with Puro when the boy who stole his mobile brings it back to him. The boy, who seems to be good at drawing, 'takes' Todd's pens and runs away. Because of the festivities Puro and Todd are late for work, but when they arrive at the call centre, one of the agents, Asha, has taken care of everything. Todd decides that his approach of making the Indian workers more American has not worked; he changes his strategy and decides to make the agents feel comfortable instead. In order to motivate them he promises to order the products they like best as a reward.
8	0:46:50 – 0:54:33	**Todd's Speech**
		As always Todd passes the remains of his lunch over the wall in the morning. At the call centre things have changed – it now looks Indian! Todd promotes Asha to Puro's assistant manager. The MPI has dropped to an incredible 6:33! The next part of the training begins: language roleplays. For a change Todd has to dance Indian style.
9	0:54:34 – 1:02:29	**The Other Gharapuri**
		The free samples that Todd has ordered have been shipped to a different Gharapuri – a three-hour drive plus ferry trip! Todd and Asha make the journey in order to retrieve the shipment. In the taxi Asha explains the significance of Kali – the goddess of destruction - to Todd. He asks for a sign of her powers. Later they learn that the ferry which was to take them back has exploded. Todd and Asha need a room to stay the night.
10	1:02:30 – 1:13:10	**Holiday in Goa**
		Apparently the only accommodation the hotel can offer Todd and Asha is the Kamasutra suite. Asha is infuriated because her parents must not find out about her and Todd. After a short argument Todd and Asha spend the night together. Back in Gharapuri Asha puts a Bollywood ringtone on Todd's mobile so that he always knows when she is calling. Just as Todd wants to give the kid some pens, he steals his mobile again. After work Todd and Asha meet at the market; they talk about their future prospects. Asha is afraid of being seen with Todd in indecent situations as she has been engaged since she is four to the son of good friends. The night with Todd was a 'Holiday in Goa'. Before she leaves, Asha passes a secret message to Todd.

Chapter	Time	Characters / Action
11	1:13:11 – 1:17:04	**An Invitation**
		When Todd is back in the garden of Aunt Ji's house one of the people to whom he always gives food motions him to follow. Todd follows his host through the dirty and narrow streets of Gharapuri. When they arrive at their destination, Todd is invited to eat with the family. The boy who has stolen his mobile brings it back again – this time with an Indian design on it.
12	1:17:05 – 1:24:53	**Dave!**
		When Todd and Dave, who has come to India on short notice, arrive at the call centre, it is flooded. As the computers are not working anymore Todd tells everybody to put them on the roof. The computers work again – the call centre is up and running! And Todd's team finally hits the 6.00 MPI target! Despite their success Dave informs Todd that the call centre is going to be moved from India to China, where the workforce is even cheaper.
13	1:24:54 – 1:31:06	**The third eye**
		In a bar for call centre agents Todd informs his people about the new situation. Except for Puro everybody is confident that they will find a new job as they are very well trained now. Puro fears that his future parents-in-law will hear about his unemployment and will thus marry their daughter to another man. Under false pretences Asha and Todd leave the bar. A friend has given Asha the key to his apartment, where they can spend their last hours together.
14	1:31:07 – 1:35:55	**The Return**
		Dave wants Todd to go immediately to Shanghai to train the new agents. Todd decides against this offer and installs Puro as the boss in Shanghai. Back in Seattle Todd is in his (bare) apartment. His mobile rings with a Bollywood ringtone.
15	1:35:56 – 1:38:54	**End credits**

QUESTIONS ON THE FILM

Having read the plot summary you now have an idea of what the film is about. In order to engage further with the film consider the following questions in the light of your knowledge of the film so far and your expectations.

- What do you expect from a film with the title *Outsourced?*
- As a marketing director how would you advertise the film and who would be your target group?
- Why do you think this film was made a topic for *Zentralabitur?*
- What aspects of the film are you particularly interested in?
- How would you feel if you had to go to India?
- What aspects of Indian life might an American find strange?
- What aspects of American life might an Indian find strange?
- Do you think the love story between Asha and Todd will have a happy ending?
- Could you imagine marrying an Indian? Why (not)?
- Do you think it is possible to learn to love somebody?
- Do you believe people can work efficiently when put under extreme time pressure?
- Imagine Todd and Puri meet again after years. What might they say to each other?
- What message do you think the film wants to convey?
- Discuss whether a film like this can influence people's attitude in a lasting way.

PRE-VIEWING ACTIVITIES

Outsourcing in a Global World

1 Explain the mind-map.

2 Are there any keywords in the mind-map you consider particularly striking? Why?
Explain in your group how the word is connected to globalisation.

3 Add more keywords to the mind-map and explain your decision to include each word.

4 Work with a partner and define the term 'outsourcing'.

5 Discuss the pros and cons of outsourcing in the context of globalisation in your group.

6 Divide your class into three groups. Each group works on one of the cartoons and presents their results to the rest of the class.

a 1 Describe the cartoon.

2 Explain the message of the cartoon.

3 Discuss what the father and the girl might consider to be the advantages and disadvantages of outsourcing.

b 1 Describe the cartoon.

2 Explain the message of the cartoon.

3 Discuss: Can there be a 'regular match' between localism and globalisation?

c 1 Describe the cartoon.

2 Explain the message of the cartoon.

3 Discuss: How can traditionalism and modernism be combined?

Approaching India

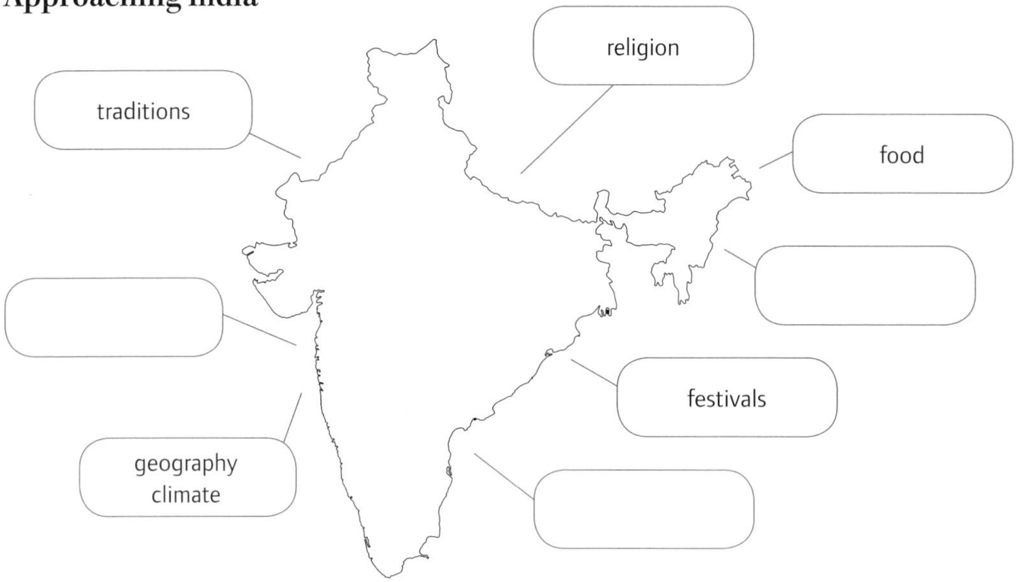

1 What do you know about India?

2 Many companies have relocated their services to India. Why do you think India has become a favourite country for outsourcing?

3 **Project:** In expert groups, plan a presentation for your classmates on the aspects mentioned in the mind map above. You are free to choose the mode of presentation (e.g. power point, transparency, handout, poster, …).

Outsourced – DVD Covers

1 Describe the different features of the cover.

2 Outline what expectations are raised with regard to the content/topic/genre of the film.

3 Comment on these expectations on the basis of your knowledge of the film (cf. plot p. 6).

4 Compare the German cover to the American version: www.outsourcedthemovie.com
What similarities or differences do you see?

5 Based on your knowledge of the film so far, discuss which cover you find more fitting.
Which one do you consider more likely to attract potential viewers?

WHILE-VIEWING ACTIVITIES

00:03:46

00:02:56

Dave in Seattle – Conversation with Todd

Watch sequence [00:01:40 – 00:04:05]

Don't forget to start your viewing log (see pp. 45 f.) to keep track of the action as well as of striking filmic devices.

1 **Close viewing:** Watch the extract of the film, paying attention to what Dave says about the necessity of outsourcing Todd's branch to India. Complete the sentences.

a When Dave learns that Todd likes Asian food he ……………

b Dave informs Todd that there will be a restructuring for ……………

c They want to …………… the whole department.

d Dave is convinced that the savings ……………

e When Todd is skeptical about language problems abroad, Dave informs him about …………… training.

f When it comes to telling the employees about losing their jobs, Dave ……………

g Dave tells Todd that his new job in India is ……………

h Moreover, Dave encourages Todd to stay with the company and promises him that ……………

i Dave thinks it is not a good idea for Todd to quit because ……………

j According to Dave, Todd's tasks in India are ……………

k The new manager is going to get ……………………………………

l The new manager's salary is worth the salary of ……………………………………

2 Explain to what extent the filmic devices underline the implications of outsourcing.

3 Compare Dave's and Todd's attitudes.

4 Evaluate Dave's and Todd's opinions on outsourcing.

Changing Offices

00:01:26

00:19:09

1 Compare the two offices.

2 Discuss where you would rather work and why.

Does Accent Matter?

Watch sequence [00:21:42 – 00:24:04]

Fill in your viewing log as you watch the film as you might need your notes and findings for future reference.

1 **Close viewing:** Watch the extract of the film and tick the correct statements. More than one statement is correct. Watch the extract twice.

- ☐ The aim of the training is for the Indians to achieve a better understanding of American culture.
- ☐ Todd is convinced that the MPI decreases proportionally to an increase in customer satisfaction.
- ☐ Asha prefers her pronunciation of English to Todd's.
- ☐ The call center agents have to pretend to be in Chicago because American customers disapprove of outsourcing.
- ☐ Asha approves of many Americans' attitude of not being keen on outsourcing on the one hand but still buying products from China.

00:23:30

00:23:58

2 Outline the reasons for the training by making a flow chart.

3 Analyse to what extent filmic devices help to emphasize the contrast between American and Indian culture. Pay special attention to camera work and setting.

4 Explain why Todd thinks that selling products the American way is more successful.

5 Comment on Todd's assessment that Americans want to buy from American speaking people: is it true?

6 Discuss whether Todd is a good teacher. Give reasons for your answer.

7 Discuss in what respect this sequence could be considered a key scene as far as presenting the main topic of the film is concerned: the clash of cultures.

Holy Cow!

Watch sequence [00:27:07– 00:28:18]

Don't forget your viewing log. How does the film go on conveying its main topic to the audience?

1 **Close viewing:** Watch the extract and then complete the following sentences.

- **a** Todd explains that many Americans wear ....
- **b** Many Americans eat a lot of beef and like to ....
- **c** This ritual derives from ....
- **d** Manmit wonders why the cows ....
- **e** Todd explains that they brand cows when ....
- **f** Asha advises Todd to ....

2 Analyse the function of the sequence with reference to the development of Todd's character in the film.

INFOBOX	Green Bay Packers Cheese Hats

Item H402, i. e. the **Green Bay Packers cheese hats**: The **Green Bay Packers** are a football team from Green Bay, Wisconsin, which is referred to as the 'Dairy State'. Because of the **cheese hats** they wear, the nickname for Green Bay Packers fans is 'Cheeseheads'.

3 Explain Todd's reaction when asked about item H402.

4 Describe the atmosphere at the end of the lesson.

The Rubber Problem

00:30:15

Watch sequence [00:29:36 – 00:30:20]

1 Explain the misunderstanding between the American grandmother and the Indian call center agent.

2 Discuss to what extent the rubber/eraser misunderstanding illustrates difficulties related to outsourcing.

3 Taking into consideration all three training sequences, state whether your opinion on Todd as a teacher has undergone a change. Give reasons for your answer.

Todd – An American in India

00:48:27

Take a look at the still and watch sequence [00:50:20 – 00:53:34]

Make notes in your viewing log.

1 Explain the connection between cultural adjustment and economic success.

2 As a teacher, what does Todd expect of his pupils?

3 As a pupil, how does Todd behave?

4 Outline the development of Todd's cultural understanding as portrayed in the previous four sequences.

Holi

1 Do research on the traditional Indian festival *Holi*.

Watch sequence [00:38:04 – 00:41:55]

Note your important findings in your viewing log.

2 Explain how the use of filmic devices creates tension in the sequence.

00:38:04

3 Analyse what makes Todd take part in the *Holi* festival.

4 Explain why the director decided to get Todd involved in the *Holi* festival at this stage of the film.

5 Analyse the meaning of the bath sequence.

00:48:27

6 **Creative writing:** Write down Todd's thoughts and feelings in the form of an interior monologue/ stream-of-consciousness when taking the bath.

Behind the Wall

00:16:44

1 Describe the walled-in garden.

2 Outline your impression of life 'behind the wall'.

Watch sequence [00:16:40 – 00:17:57]

Continue to fill in your viewing log.

3 Analyse how your impression is supported by the use of filmic devices.

4 Contrast the two places on either side of the wall.

5 Assess the wall in its filmic and its literal dimension.

INFOBOX | **India in Close-Up**

Official name	Republic of India
Area	3,287,240 km² (7th in world)
Capital	New Delhi
Political System	Parliamentary democracy (the world's largest)
Currency	Indian rupee
Population	1,2 billion (2nd in world)
Urban/rural population	29 %/71 %
Access to improved water	89 %
Access to improved sanitation	33 %
Life expectancy	64 years
Infant mortality (to age 1 year)	57 per 1000 live births
Under-5-mortality	72 per 1000
Underweight children under 5	46 %
Literacy rate	65 % (76 % for males, 54 % for females)
Primary school	83 % of primary school children enrolled
Population with phones	15 %
Internet users	11 %
Working population	487,6 million
Domestic workers	14 million
Women employed in rural areas/in cities	31 %/11 %
Child labourers	between 10.25 % to 19.90 % of all Indian children aged 9–15
People below poverty line	about 260 million
Number of people living in slums	150 million
Average monthly wage	112 USD
People living on less than 1 USD per day	about 336 million

6 Using the facts and figures in the box 'India in Close-Up' to help you, prepare a short talk on poverty and employment in India.

7 To what extent are your findings mirrored in the film?

Watch sequence [1:13:10 – 1:15:13]

Make notes in your viewing log.

1:15:01

8 In the thought bubbles, write down Todd's thoughts and feelings while following Sanjeev.

9 Explain the function of this sequence using your knowledge on employment and poverty in India.

Watch the rest of the sequence: [1:15:14 – 1:16:38]

10 Outline what happens in the last part of the sequence.

11 Considering the information in the box, outline why it is important for Sanjeev to invite Todd to have dinner with his family.

12 Add the new information you have gathered to the mind map.

INFOBOX	**Hospitality**

Offering **hospitality** is fundamental to Hindu culture and providing food and shelter to a needy stranger was a traditional duty of the householder. The unexpected guest is called the atithi, literally meaning 'without a set time'. [...] There are many stories regarding the benefits of offering a suitable reception and the sins that accrue from neglecting one's guests. Tradition teaches that, no matter how poor one is, one should always offer three items: sweet words, a sitting place, and refreshments (at least a glass of water). The flower garland is offered to special guests and dignitaries, as a symbol of loving exchange.

From: ISKCON Educational Services, 2004

The Kid

00:21:34

00:43:19

00:43:46

1:07:13

1:16:51

1 Describe the stills. What do they reveal about the kid?

2 Work together with a partner. Divide the stills between you and analyse their composition. What do viewers get to see? What is the effect of this?

3 Share your findings with your partner and explain how the relationship between Todd and the kid develops. Visualize your findings by means of a graph, a flow chart or another kind of illustration.

MacDonnells

Watch sequence [00:35:00 – 00:37:01]

1 Which burger comes closest to a cheeseburger?

2 What does INDIA stand for?

3 How did the man in the story outsource his own job?

4 What jobs are being outsourced to India?

5 What advice does the other expat give to Todd?

00:36:51

6 To what extent does the still reflect the advice symbolically?

7 **Project:** Do an Internet research on the food McDonald's, Kentucky Fried Chicken and Subway offer in India. Compare the menus to the ones in Germany. Prepare a presentation.

The Minor Characters

INFOBOX | **Character**

A character is a person in a fictional text. Characters can be presented through their actions, speech and thoughts as well as through description. Characters can be classified according to their importance as **main characters** or **minor characters** and according to their type as round characters or flat characters. A **round character** has several character traits and behaves in a life-life way, usually developing in the course of the story. A **flat character** only has a limited number of traits and may even just represent a singly quality. While main characters are usually round characters, flat characters are usually minor characters. The way in which the characters are presented is called characterization.

1 Outline the function of the three minor characters in the film with reference to the main character

– as concerns the development of the plot.

– in connection to the message(s) conveyed by the film.

2 Imagine the director had cut out one or all of these three characters. How would this have impacted the storyline? Fill in the chart completing the if-clauses.

If the director had cut out

Sanjeev	
the kid	
the expat	

3 Which other minor characters can you identify? Describe them and explain their function.

Kali

1 Describe the picture of Kali.

2 What is your personal impression of this goddess?

3 Do some research on the goddess Kali.

4 Re-evaluate your initial impression of Kali.

Watch sequence [00:55:00 – 00:55:40]

5 Outline how Todd reacts to the goddess in the car.

6 Describe Asha's attitude towards Kali.

7 Explain why Kali appears at this stage of the film.

8 The goddess Kali appears throughout the film. In your group, discuss why the filmmakers decided on this.

POST-VIEWING ACTIVITIES

1 Life Lessons in a Global Marketplace

MATT ZOLLER SEITZ

Outsourced, in which a Seattle call center manager named Todd (Josh Hamilton) is fired and then dispatched to India as a consultant to train his own replacement, is a wonderful surprise.

At first it threatens to be just another fish-out-of-water story. The film's director, John Jeffcoat, and his co-writer, George Wing, hit expected marks, from the moment when a street urchin swipes the hero's cellphone to the bit where Todd learns why Indians don't eat with their left hand to the scene where Todd realizes that his sharpest employee, an outspoken young woman named Asha (Ayesha Dharker), is gorgeous and has a crush on him.

Gratifyingly, though, the filmmakers treat Todd's story as a springboard for a smart look at the effect of cultural difference on work, friendship and love, and the global economy's impact on national and personal identity.

Todd, being American, has no sense of himself as an American. He has an allergic reaction to Indian culture (embodied by the intestinal distress he suffers after eating local food). He is also taken aback by Indians' emphasis on family ties and social obligations, and they in turn are politely aghast at Todd's disconnection from his own relatives.

Todd's trainee, the polite, 40-ish Puro (Asif Basra), lives with his parents and is surprised that Todd lives alone and rarely visits his own mother. He insists that Todd forgo his prearranged hotel room and stay at his home, where his mom cooks up a storm and grills Todd on why he isn't married yet.

Todd is initially concerned with improving his employees' minutes-per-call rating and going home. He's bored by his job and can't believe that his employees like the kitschy Americana (including Green Bay Packers cheese hats) sold through his company's catalog.

But during an impulsive trip to a McDonald's knockoff that doesn't serve beef, he meets a fellow American (Larry Pine, in a brilliant cameo) who advises him: 'I was resisting India. Once I gave in, I did much better.'

Todd has an epiphany while wading into a local water tank (photographed, with cross-cultural wit, to suggest a baptism). He also comes to understand Indians' comfort with images of Kali, the Hindu goddess of creation, preservation and destruction. Todd learns that change can be negative, positive or simply neutral, and what matters is how one reacts to it.

The film shows that individuals in every nation are nearly powerless before the global economy, a force that shatters tradition and compels

2 *dispatch sb./sth.* send sb./sth. somewhere

4 *fish-out-of-water story* a story about sb. who doesn't fit into the situation they are in

6 *urchin* a homeless child

6 *swipe sth. (infml)* to steal sth.

10 *springboard* sth. that helps you start doing sth.

14 *intestinal* adj. of 'intestine' (the tube in your body that carries food from your stomach)

15 *be taken aback* be very surprised or shocked

16 *be aghast* be shocked

20 *forgo sth. (fml)* not to do or have sth. that you want

21 *cook up a storm* evoke trouble

21 *grill sb. on sth.* ask sb. a lot of questions

25 *Americana* American souvenirs/artefacts

25 *Green Bay Packers cheese hat* cf. Infobox p. 18

27 *knockoff (infml)* copy

30 *epiphany* a sudden realization

33 *preservation* the act of preventing sth. from being harmed or damaged people to think of themselves as self-interested free agents. This pragmatic point of view is articulated by Asha, who rhetorically asks Todd why it's necessary for Indian call-center workers to pose as Americans while selling cheap junk made in China.

The key to survival is adaptability, a quality demonstrated by every major character in *Outsourced* — particularly Todd, who adapts to his hosts' culture and language and makes them more invested in their jobs by rewarding efficiency gains with products from the company's catalog.

In its modest way, *Outsourced* may be unique: a charming culture-clash romance that could be taught in business schools.

45 *unique* the only one of its kind

From: The New York Times, *28 September 2007*

1 **Reading for gist:** Tick the statement that best sums up the main idea of the text:

- □ *Outsourced* mainly deals with the love story between an American man and an Indian woman.
- □ *Outsourced* is mainly about a business man's experience in/with India.
- □ *Outsourced* mainly deals with cross-cultural conflicts.
- □ *Outsourced* is mainly about the Indian lifestyle.

2 **Reading for detail:** Finish the sentence by choosing the correct ending:

a According to Matt Zoller Seitz

- □ the film shows the impact globalisation can have on the individual.
- □ the film criticizes companies who operate in foreign countries.
- □ the film is a warning to those who want to do business abroad.
- □ the film explores the idea of an American finding himself in a foreign country.

b *Outsourced* is

- □ a love story.
- □ a comedy.
- □ a mixture of different genres.
- □ a tragedy.

c The critic is of the opinion that cultural difference

- □ is to be avoided.
- □ can't be avoided.
- □ is a vital part in business relations nowadays.
- □ must be achieved in business relations today.

3 Explain why Zoller Seitz considers *Outsourced* 'a wonderful surprise'.

4 Discuss: Can films like *Outsourced* make people more aware of cultural differences and their impact on the individual?

5 Can you imagine living and working in a country like India? Give reasons for your answer.

6 Write your own personal review of the film. State your overall impression and give the film a rating. Use the section *How to Write a Film Review* (p. 47) to help you with this writing project.

2 The Indian Dream: The Success of *Slumdog Millionaire* in the USA

ANAND GIRIDHARADAS

It isn't about cows or cobras, a wedding or outsourcing. It isn't about gurus or Gandhi. *Slumdog Millionaire,* in fact, may be the first world-traveling film about India in a generation to discard the old, smudged lenses for seeing this country.

Its novelty has given it a dream run in U.S. movie theaters, and last week it won best dramatic picture at the Golden Globe Awards in Los Angeles. It now is given a good shot at the Academy Awards next month, even though much of the dialogue is in Hindi.

But the film's freshness lies not just in how the West sees India. It lies, too, in how Indians see themselves. It portrays a changing India, with great realism, as something India long resisted being: a land of self-makers, where a scruffy son of the slums can hoist himself up, flout his origins, break with fate.

And that may explain the movie's strange hold over Americans. It channels to them their own Gatsbyesque fantasy of self-invention, and yet places it far enough away as to imply that it is now really someone else's fantasy. [...]

The film follows Jamal Malik, who rises from Mumbai's shantytowns to compete on the Indian version of *Who Wants to Be a Millionaire?* His life begins in a familiar, eternal India: the India of layers of humiliation, of the swirling crowd that drowns the self.

The director, Danny Boyle, shows us the many clamps on Indian selves. The arbitrary power of police officer toward citizen and gangster toward slum dweller. The schools where teachers throw books at students and lessons consist of choral echoing of the teacher's words. The slum where cooking and child-rearing and defecation are semi-public activities, and where it would be hard to develop the mental independence to question an arranged marriage or abuse by the better-born.

In Malik's environs, you don't happen to the world; the world happens to you.

But our hero has his own larger vision of life. It is, at first, a vision compelled: he and his brother are orphaned and must survive. But in time

3 *discard sth.* throw sth. away
3 *smudged* dirty
12 *scruffy* dirty, untidy
12 *hoist sth.* lift sth. heavy
12 *flout sth.* deliberately disobey a law or a rule
18 *shantytown* a poor area in or near a town where people live in cardboard houses
22 *clamp* equipment for holding things together
26 *child-rearing* the process of raising a child
26 *defecation* Darmentleerung
29 *environs*

Malik parlays that pain into a knack for succeeding, becoming a train vendor, then a tour guide to the gullible in Agra, then a tea wallah in a Mumbai office.

In India, clan is everything. But Malik needs no one. He has no parents; his brother betrays him; even the game-show host, feigning good will, deceives. In India, hierarchy rules. But Malik treats the mighty no differently from the meek, does not cower even before the police. He is that rare, but increasingly less rare, Indian creature: a man all his own.

The old restraints were formidable: family, caste, religious fatalism, byzantine bureaucracy: so many forces conspiring to keep uppity selves in check. Even today, India is no free-for-all.

But the new pull is centrifugal, toward the lonely periphery and away from the buzzing center, toward a life of one's making, in a city not one's own, in a vocation not inherited. It is the unmarried women working nights in Delhi's call centers. The divorces sprouting where acquiescence ruled. The spreading belief that destiny can, with scars and ardor, be bent.

'Why does everyone love this program?' Malik, seeing the 'Millionaire' show on television, asks a friend one day.

'It's a chance to escape, isn't it?' she replies. 'Walk into another life.'

The United States was founded with the promise of such escape. Its early settlers were fleeing restraints much like the old India's. They drove the natives away, then built a nation premised on space and self-making: a frontier land where families had their own acres, own gun, own conscience. That, at least, was the mythology.

But it has been a long time; and now, even as the myth of self-making spreads to India, a pause for second thoughts may have started in America. It was partly the crash of 2008, in which supposed masters of the universe, unsupervised, tanked the economy, then sheepishly asked to be bailed out. It was partly a dawning sense that policies that promoted the entrepreneur could forget communities and contexts. It was partly the fraying of American families, the 'joyless and anomic self-indulgence of the Me Generation,' as the writer David Foster Wallace put it.

And so as Indians sever their attachments, Americans reweave theirs. Harvard Business School now teaches courses like 'Entrepreneurship in Education Reform' to satisfy students who want to mix private and public gain. Bill Gates and Warren Buffett have argued that they owe their success to a conducive society and have resolved to give their wealth away.

Scientists, too, are pushing the self-made from their pedestal, arguing that success is social: that certain cultures breed success, that genes influence skills, that there are favorable times to be born.

'Personal explanations of success don't work,' Malcolm Gladwell writes in *Outliers*, his new book on the research. In a magazine interview, he derided 'empty models that say, you know, you can be whatever you want to be.'

'Well, actually, you can't be whatever you want to be,' Gladwell said. 'The world decides what you can and can't be.' [...]

33 *parlay skills* Fähigkeiten nutzen

33 *knack* talent

34 *vendor* person who sells sth.

34 *gullible* too ready to believe what other people tell you

34 *wallah* sb. who does a particular job or duty

37 *feign sth. (fml)* pretend

39 *meek* unterwürfig

39 *cower* duck, humble yourself

41 *restraint* restriction

42 *byzantine (fml)* very complicated

42 *uppity* hochnäsig

46 *vocation* Berufung

47 *sprout* start to grow

47 *acquiescence* agreement to do what sb. wants

48 *scar* Narbe

48 *ardor* strong admiration

54 *be premised* be based on a particular idea

60 *supervise sb.* jd. kontrollieren

60 *be bailed out* escape from an uncomfortable situation

61 *entrepreneur* Unternehmer/in

62 *fraying* annoying

63 *anomic* lacking moral standards

63 *self-indulgence* Hemmungslosigkeit

65 *sever sth.* ['sevə] *(fml)* separate sth.

65 *reweave* create again

69 *conducive* [kən'dju:sɪv] making sth. possible or likely to happen

70 *pedestal* Sockel

75 *deride sth.* mock sth.

It is roots and linkages that many Indians now seek to shed, and many Americans now seek to reclaim. And that may be the silent allure of *Slumdog Millionaire*. It is a tribute to the irrepressible self, filmed in a society now realizing it has given the self too little, watched in a society now realizing it has given the self too much.

79 *shed sth.* get rid of sth. you don't want

80 *allure* [ə'lʊə] *(fml)* the quality of being attractive and exciting

From: Indians adopt a vision under siege in America, in: The New York Times, *15 January 2009*

1 Why was the film *Slumdog Millionaire* so successful?

2 Explain what aspects the article reveals about Indian life nowadays.

3 Discuss: Can the situation presented in the film be transferred to the living conditions in the USA? To what extent?

4 Comment on the last sentence of the text. Give reasons for your opinion.

We are the masters, and you shine our shoes.

Noam Chomsky on US proposals for a New World Order

3 Godfather

ROGER WODDIS

Whatever new system
You happen to choose,
We are the masters,
And you shine our shoes.

Defeating the tyrant
Is yesterday's news:
We are the masters,
And you shine our shoes.

With hands on our hearts,
While respecting your views,
We are the masters,
And you shine our shoes.

Don't look at our lips,
See the methods we use:
We are the masters,
And you shine our shoes.

There are some that we win,
There are some that you lose
We are the masters,
And you shine our shoes.

So here is an offer
You just can't refuse:
We are the masters,
And you shine our shoes.

From: One Over the 80's. Poems from the New Statesman 1982–1992,
London: Perseverance Press

1 Describe the roles of 'we' and 'you'. What are the roles of 'we' and 'you' in relation to each other?

2 Analyse the stylistic devices the author employs in his poem.

3 Explain what view of the modern world the poem conveys.

4 Comment on the following statement:
The spread of new technologies throughout the world is not working to advance freedom. Instead it has resulted in the emancipation of market forces from social and political control. By allowing that freedom to world markets we ensure that the age of globalization will be remembered as another turn in the history of servitude.
John Gray, False Dawn. The delusions of global capitalism. *London: Granta, 1998, p. 23*

5 Compare the views expressed in the poem and in the quote above and state which one you prefer. Give reasons for your choice.

6 Think of alternative ways of structuring the economy for the benefit of more people.

4 The Impact of Outsourcing – Fishbowl Discussion

INFOBOX | **Fishbowl Discussion**

A **fishbowl** conversation is a form of dialogue that can be used when discussing topics in a large group by dividing the group into those who form the fishbowl and those who are the 'goldfish'. The advantage of a fishbowl is that it allows the entire group to participate in a conversation.

There are two different kinds of fishbowl discussions: the open and the closed fishbowl.

In an **open fishbowl**, one chair is left empty. Any member of the fishbowl can sit down on the empty chair and join the goldfish in the inner circle at any point in the discussion. When this happens, a member of the inner circle must voluntarily leave so that there is always one free chair available. The discussion unfolds with participants frequently entering and leaving the inner circle.

In a **closed fishbowl**, all chairs are filled. The moderator introduces the topic and the goldfish start discussing the topic. The audience outside listen to the discussion and take notes. When time runs out all goldfish leave the inner circle and a new group of goldfish from the fishbowl enter.

You can choose whether you want to form an open or a closed fishbowl.

Preparation

1 Divide the class into six groups.

Groups one to five are responsible for the following characters/roles:
Todd (American employee and coach)
Dave (boss)
Asha (representative of Indian employees)
American customer (alternatively Grandmother)
Paul (former colleague of Todd's who was fired)

Group six is responsible for the moderator.

2 Before you start the actual discussion, decide who is going to observe whom.

The Characters

Bearing in mind the topic of the fishbowl discussion, write a profile for 'your' character:

Who are you? What is your 'function/role' in the process of globalisation/outsourcing? To what extent do you profit from outsourcing? To what extent do you suffer under outsourcing?

How do/did you feel in certain situations?

Imagine what 'your' character wants to say to the others:

Are you thankful/angry/disappointed? Do you want to reproach or blame anybody? Do you want to justify yourself for what you have done to somebody else? What do you want to ask the others?

The Moderator

1 Before the discussion:

Be prepared to

- welcome the participants to the discussion and explain what it will be about.
- stimulate the discussion by asking the participants questions that 'force' them to take a stance, to explain their motives for certain actions etc.
- explain the rules, namely:
  The members of the fishbowl are not allowed to communicate with the goldfish.
  The goldfish should first introduce their characters: Who are you? What happened to you?
  The goldfish are not allowed to interrupt each other.
  Rules of good behaviour must be followed.

2 During the discussion:

- Get the discussion going by calling on one of the participants to start the first round.
- Open the second round by calling on one of the participants to start his/her statement (see topic of discussion).
- Make sure that each goldfish/character is allowed to speak.
- In your role as moderator you must call the group to order and interrupt any participants who do not stick to the topic.
- You are responsible for the flow of the conversation, so be prepared to ask questions (see above).

3 At the end of the discussion:

- Give a short summary of what the goldfish have said.
- Thank the participants for the discussion.

Evaluation

1 First the participants say how they felt in their role as 'goldfish'.

2 The observers now give feedback to the participants of the discussion. This can be done in small groups.

3 For feedback to be successful, it is very important to first focus on what somebody did well and then to say what he/she can do in order to improve his/her performance.

The observation sheet (→ p. 35) might help the observers to give feedback.

	Comment	Overall impression
Language		
Fluency		
Pronunciation/loudness/speed		
Grammar		
Choice of words		
Content		
Substantiality of statements/answers		
Accordance between statements and character as presented in the film		
Ability to answer to questions		
Communication		
Listening to others		
Showing interest in the other participants' statements		
Ability to connect one's own ideas to those of the previous speaker		

5 Outsourcing

Das Ende des indischen Callcenter-Wunders

VOLKER MÜLLER

Mediation

Your school is participating in an international project on economic trends. Your group, consisting of students from France, the Netherlands, Poland and Austria, has chosen to work on the topic 'Outsourcing to India'.

After reading the article below, you decide that it suits your group's topic perfectly.

So you prepare to present your information to the other members of your group, referring to past and present developments in outsourcing to India, problems the outsourcing industry is faced with and measures taken to solve these problems.

To make sure that all members of your group understand the information given, you prepare your presentation in English.

Die Wirtschaftskrise ist nur scheinbar eine Chance für indische IT-Dienstleister: Zwar können Unternehmen aus der westlichen Welt viel Geld durch Outsourcing nach Indien sparen. Doch die Kundschaft aus den USA und Westeuropa spart neuerdings sogar beim Sparen. Indische Anbieter setzen nun auf eine neue Strategie. [...]

Binnen 30 Jahren wuchs die einst nur 2,5 Millionen Einwohner zählende Stadt zum Moloch mit heute 6,5 Millionen Menschen. SAP und IBM siedelten sich hier an, Tata Consultancy Services, Wipro und Infosys. Sie bauten Campus um Campus, glasverspiegelte Scheußlichkeiten moderner Büroarchitektur, hermetisch abgeriegelte Kühlkammern für Technik und Menschen, in denen der märchenhafte Aufstieg Indiens zu einer der weltweit führenden IT-Nationen gelang.

Im Minutentakt ergießen sich Busladungen von Mitarbeitern über die weitläufigen Gelände der IT-Konzerne. Auf mehr als 800.000 Mitarbeiter ist die Branche landesweit gewachsen, mehr als 46,3 Milliarden Dollar Umsatz erzielte sie im Jahr 2008, ermittelte der Branchenverband Nasscom. Ihr Geschäft: Sie nehmen amerikanischen und europäischen Firmen teure, IT-gestützte Verwaltungsarbeiten ab – von der elektronischen Reisekostenabrechnung über Dokumentenarchivierung bis hin zur Personalverwaltung. Das spart Milliarden. Dank niedriger indischer Löhne ist es für beide Seiten ein attraktives Geschäft. Nirgendwo sonst auf der Welt wird mit Outsourcing mehr Geld verdient als in Bangalore.

Vorbei. Seit 2008 herrscht Trübsal. Die Flut schlechter Nachrichten will nicht abreißen. Die Kundschaft aus den USA und Westeuropa spart neuerdings sogar am Sparen. Gerade einmal vier bis sieben Prozent, auf 48 bis 50 Milliarden Dollar Umsatz, werde die Branche im laufenden Finanzjahr bis März 2010 wachsen, rechnet Nasscom vor. So wenig Wachstum war nie. Im jüngst abgeschlossenen Jahr meldete die Branche noch ein Plus von 16 Prozent, davor sogar 29 Prozent. [...]

Umsteuern in der Krise

Ein neues Geschäftsmodell soll den indischen Dienstleistern nun helfen, künftige Krisen besser zu meistern. Denn: „Die Preise für Outsourcing werden nicht mehr steigen. Wir können schon froh sein, wenn wir sie auf dem heutigen Niveau halten können", sagt Nataraja Chandrasekaran, Vize-Chef des Branchenprimus TCS. Die Zukunft liege in margenträchtigeren Geschäften, etwa der umfassenden Beratung oder der Übernahme ganzer Geschäftsabläufe. „Wir werden zunehmend das tun, was IBM oder Accenture heute bereits tun", sagt der TCS-Manager.

Der Vergleich mit US-Gigant IBM zeigt die Schwächen der einheimischen Unternehmen: Die etwa 90.000 IBM-Mitarbeiter in Indien erzielen pro Kopf dreimal soviel Umsatz wie die Angestellten von Wipro. Seit Jahren bereits konzentriert sich der US-Konzern darauf, langfristige Geschäfte mit hoher Wertschöpfung abzuschließen, während sich indische Unternehmen lange auf einfache Tätigkeiten konzentriert haben. So landete schließlich auch das attraktivste Geschäft im Heimatmarkt, ein 800 Millionen Dollar schwerer Fünfjahresvertrag mit Vodafone, bei IBM.

Tatsächlich erzielen TCS und seine heimischen Wettbewerber nur fünf Prozent ihrer Umsätze mit besonders anspruchsvollen Geschäften, westliche Konkurrenten hingegen die Hälfte. „Um langfristig und nachhaltig das Wachstum der vergangenen Jahre wieder zu erreichen, können die Inder nicht einfach nur Allerwelts-Dienstleistungen anbieten", urteilt auch Kapil Dev Singh, Landeschef Indien des Marktforschers IDC. Das Problem: Für höherwertige Aufträge fehlt den indischen Unternehmen derzeit noch Personal und Erfahrung.

HCL Technologies, einer der fünf Großen der Branche, geht nun ins Risiko. Der Dienstleister will sich nicht mehr auf eng begrenzte Aufgaben beschränken. Vielmehr will HCL ganze Geschäftsprozesse seiner Kunden beflügeln, etwa die gesamte Logistikkette oder das Online-Geschäft. Dafür stellt HCL Heerscharen zusätzlicher Experten bereit und trägt einen Großteil des Kostenrisikos. Erst wenn sich der Erfolg einstellt, profitiert auch der Dienstleister. Ein riskantes Geschäft, denn nicht immer ist klar, ob sich die versprochenen Sparerfolge einstellen. Eines aber gewinnt HCL mit Sicherheit: Erfahrung.

From: Welt Online, *4 August 2009*

EXAM TASKS

The following tasks are formulated as possible exam tasks. You can choose one or more from each section to prepare for an upcoming exam.

I Comprehension (text comprehension and definition)

1 Summarize the plot in no more than 150 words.

2 Outline the concept of outsourcing as depicted in the film.

II Analysis (text analysis, text comparison and stylistic devices)

1 Explain the message of the film.

2 Contrast the working conditions in India with the working conditions in the U.S. as depicted in the film.

3 Compare and contrast Todd's and Asha's tactics to improve work in the call centre.

4 Analyse Auntie Ji's role as a host.

III Comment/Composition/Creative Writing (discussion, comment, evaluation and text production)

1 Justify Dave's decision to outsource the company to India.

2 Write a characterization of Todd.

3 Comment on Todd's behaviour when he arrives in India.

4 Evaluate Todd's role as a boss in India.

5 Discuss the impact of outsourcing on the Indian workers, paying special attention to Puro and Asha.

6 One day, Todd is caught in Holi, the celebration of colours. Write the diary entry he writes at the end of the day.

7 Comment on Dave's statement 'China is the new India. Twenty heads for the price of one.'

8 Todd is back home and wants to contact Asha. Write Todd's letter to Asha about his time in India and his present life.

9 Discuss Todd and Asha's chances as a couple.

10 Back in Seattle, Todd contacts Puro in China. Speculate on a possible conversation they might have and write it down.

11 Write an alternative ending to the film.

SELECTED TERMS FOR FILM ANALYSIS

Camera range/kinds of shot	The distance between camera and object
close shot	In a **close shot** a person's face, shoulders and part of his/her arm are shown.
close-up 	An entire human face from chin or lower neck to top of head fills the frame. Shows the finest nuances of expression.
extreme close-up 	Parts of the face (or object) fill the entire frame.
full shot 	Includes the entire body of a character and not much else. The **full shot** is used to emphasize action and the constellation of characters.
long shot 	Characters and surroundings are shown from a distance and in their entirety. It is usually used to introduce a new setting (see **establishing shot**) to show characters in relation to the action, to show movement over large distances, or to juxtapose different characters within one frame.
medium shot 	Characters and surroundings are shown at a moderate size, with characters seen from mid-body up. It is usually chosen to show one or two characters in action.

Camera perspective	
establishing shot	A **long shot** that establishes a setting, scene or mood; frequently used at the beginning of a scene.
over-the-shoulder shot	A shot taken with the camera placed behind a character who is only partially seen, looking over his/her shoulder. Usually used in dialogue scenes, showing the dialogue partner from the second character's point of view.
point-of-view shot	Also known as 'subjective camera'. A shot taken with the camera placed approximately where the characters' eyes would be in order to depict a scene from the visual or emotional perspective of one of the characters.
shot/reverse shot **reverse-angle shot** 	A **shot/reverse shot** is an **over-the-shoulder shot** followed by a **reverse-angle shot**. A **reverse-angle shot** is a shot in which the angle is opposite to that in the preceding shot.
Camera angle	
eye-level shot/ straight-on angle 	A shot filmed at eye level.
high-angle shot 	A shot filmed from above the object; may be used to diminish the character's importance.
low-angle shot 	Filmed from below the object, a **low-angle shot** may be used to underline the importance or power of a character or object. Shown as a **point-of-view shot**, it indicates fear or respect on the part of the character viewing a particular scene.

Camera movement	
crane shot 	A shot filmed from a crane that can move the camera in any direction. It is almost always linked to another movement of the camera, such as a **pan** or **tilt**, in which case it becomes a compound movement.
hand-held camera	A filming technique in which the camera is held by the operator during a take.
pan/panning shot 	The camera moves horizontally from left to right or vice versa (**pan** right or **pan** left). A **panning shot** is often used to follow a character's movement or to indicate a **point-of-view shot** with the character looking around or searching for something.
tilt/tilt shot	The camera moves vertically upward or downward. A **tilt shot** is often used to indicate height or follow a character or object moving up or downwards, e.g. a leaf dropping.
tracking shot 	Camera movement in which the entire camera is moved either forward, backward, laterally, or in a circular or irregular pattern. The camera is placed on a movable device (a camera dolly) moving along pre-laid tracks or is moved freely along a level surface (hand-held camera or steady cam). In a **tracking shot**, the camera range may either remain constant, following along next to or behind a moving character or object, or it may be used to get closer to or further away from the target object in a manner similar to a **zoom** shot. Usually used to indicate steady movement through the setting, e.g. indicating a character running or two characters walking together.
zoom 	The stationary camera appears to approach a character or object by **zooming in** or to move farther away by **zooming out**.

Editing terms	The arrangement of shots in a structured sequence
cross-cutting/ parallel action	Also known as parallel editing. An editing technique that alternates shots of two or more actions occurring in different places at the same time. Usually used to follow multiple plot lines, to compare or to juxtapose different actions or settings, or to show different reactions to a particular event.
cut	Transition from one shot to another. The most basic editing technique for connecting two shots within a scene and between scenes.
jump-cut	A (very) abrupt transition from one shot to another eleminating one strip of action and creating an effect of disorientation or rapid movement.
match cut	A technique in which two shots are linked by the same acting or by some form of visual parallelism. The two shots seem to continue uninterrupted, e.g. one door closing and then another door opening. **Match cuts** can be used to underline a connection between two separate elements. Often used to create a smooth flow between two scenes or, if using the same character in the action, to mark the passing of time.
dissolve	A transition between two shots created by gradually overlapping the last shot of a scene with the first shot of the next scene. This is done by superimposing a **fade-out** onto a **fade-in** of equal length. Often this transition is used to underline the connection between two scenes or to indicate a change of location or the passing of time.
fade-in **fade-out**	A transition between two shots. The last image of one scene gradually disappears from the screen (**fade-out**) to be replaced by a monochrome screen, and the first shot of the next scene gradually brightens from a blank screen to the whole image (**fade-in**). Often used to indicate a passing of time (e.g. from night to day), or to mark the beginning and end of a dream sequence (**flashback** or **flash-forward**).
flashback	A filmed sequence that goes back in narrative time to show events that took place earlier than the present-time of the film. Usually used to provide expository material and to underline the feelings and motives of characters.
flash-forward	A filmed sequence that moves forward in narrative time to show events that take place later than the present-time of the film. Usually used to underline the presence of an omniscient narrator, a **flash-forward** shows the consequences of a certain action that the characters are still unaware of. It gives the audience the impression of knowing more than the characters.
Additional film terms	
arc shot	Camera movement in which the entire camera moves around a subject or object in a circle.
backlighting	Filming a person or event against a background of light, e.g. the sun. It may produce an idealized, sometimes romantic effect.
camera operator	The person behind the camera(s); in major productions, the head of the camera team is usually called the director of photography.
cast	All actors who appear in a film.

clapboard (US)/ **clapperboard** (GB) 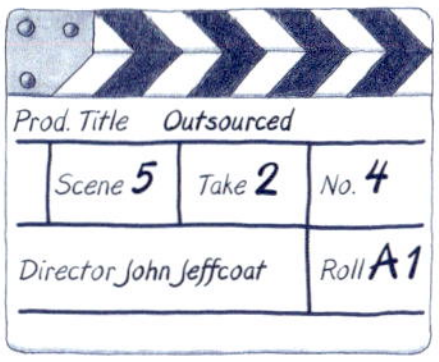	A small board which gives information about a film: e.g. the director, the director of photography, the scene, take number, date and time. It is filmed at the beginning of each take. It helps to identify all takes and cuts down continuity errors.
credits	The list of people who were involved in the making of a film or television programme.
director	The person responsible for the artistic production of a film, involving all its creative elements, e.g. camerawork, editing, and the actors' interpretation of their roles.
editor	(verb: edit) The person responsible for putting the camera shots together and arranging them into a finished product.
fade	Transition between two shots. The last image gradually disappears from the screen (**fade-out**) to be replaced by a monochrome screen, and the first shot of the next screen gradually brightens from a blank screen to the whole image (**fade-in**).
footage	A length of film made for TV or cinema.
frame	A single image of the film.
insert (shot)	A detail shot which quickly gives visual information necessary to understand the meaning of a scene, e.g. a newspaper page or a physical detail.
lighting	The creation of controlled illumination upon a scene or object to be filmed and thus the ultimate tool of the cinematographer. Light sources may be natural or artificial or both. If natural, the light may be directed onto the scene by reflecting devices. If artificial, it is of course aimed at the specific target area designated by the director of photography and channelled through the use of such devices as cookies, flags, and doors. The light may also be diffused or it may be sharply focused. If, as might be said, cinematography is painting with light, lighting is the palette which the painter uses. Though methods for lighting a scene are highly varied, the one most commonly used in conventional practice is known as the 'Three-Point Lighting System'.
high-key lighting **low-key lighting**	The intensity and sharpness of light and corresponding shadow (or lack of this) which illuminates a scene is described as being either **high** or **low key**. This is true irrespective of whether the film is monochromatic or in colour. Lighting that creates comparatively little contrast between the light and dark areas of the shot is **high-key**, lighting that creates strong contrast between the light and dark areas of the shot is **low-key lighting**.
location	See: set.

mise-en-scène	Literally translated from French, the phrase means 'put upon the stage'; otherwise known simply as 'staging'. In film-making the term has come to mean the totality of how the director designs and sets in motion a given scene. All films use essentially the same techniques and processes. However, each individual film employs all of the variable elements of production provided by the technology available in its own distinct way. The elements generally used to define and analyse **mise-en-scène** are: setting, actor placement, actor movement, actor interpretation (ideally, but not always a collaboration between director and actor), camera movement, costumes and make-up.
motion picture/movie	US and Canadian terms for film.
producer	The person responsible for the overall organization, especially the financing and marketing, of a film or television production.
scene	A shot or series of shots that deal with a single action (see also **sequence**).
score	Film music.
screenplay	The script of a film or television show, usually including dialogue as well as rough descriptions of the setting, camera distance, camera movements, etc.
sequence	A part of a film dealing with one or more scenes that form a single continuous episode.
set	The site or location where a film is being shot.
shot	A single piece of film, however long or short, taken by a single camera without cuts.
soundtrack	The audio equivalent of the picture or image track, the **soundtrack** contains all the audio information which accompanies the film: dialogue, music, sound effects, etc.
still	A single photograph or shot from a film.
storyboard	A **storyboard** is a useful tool in the creation of any media production. It is a series of sketches or still photographs that show how the different shots might look when filmed. It almost looks like a comic book of the film.
take	A single attempt to film a shot. Though sometimes confused with **shot**, there can in fact be an unlimited number of takes of the same shot until either the director is satisfied or the producer calls a halt.
top shot	Extreme **high-angle shot** where the camera looks straight down.
voice-over	An off-screen voice that gives the audience necessary background information. It is often used in documentaries. In a narrative film, this technique often implies a first-person or omniscient narrator's point of view.
wipe	Transitional device in which shot B seemingly moves in either screen direction across shot A, thus effectively wiping off shot A and replacing it.

WORKING WITH A FILM VIEWING LOG

You are probably used to keeping a reading log when studying a novel. When studying a film, it is even more important to take notes during the viewing process for future reference, as it is more difficult to go back to different parts of the film.

Before viewing
Find out all you can about the film you are going to see:

What genre does it belong to (e.g. feature film, documentary, video clip, newscast, commercial)? What country does it come from? When was it made? Are you going to see it in the original language (with or without subtitles), or is it a dubbed version? Was it made for television or for the cinema?

While viewing
Pay close attention to how visual and audio elements influence your reaction to the film:

- **Characters:** How does the film show you who the main characters are? What information do you get about them? What is their relationship to each other? What impression do they make on you, and why? Watch for facial expressions and body language that may convey important signals.

- **Setting:** How does the film let you know where the plot is set? What impression do you get of the setting? How do colour, music, lighting, background noise contribute to this impression?

- **Plot:** Is the plot introduced gradually (e.g. while the titles are being shown) or does the story begin in the middle and make the viewer draw conclusions based on indirect clues? Does it use flashbacks (or flash-forwards), or is the story told chronologically? Does the point of view of one character dominate, or does the film jump from one character to another? Is there one main plot, or does the film tell a series of loosely connected episodes? Are special effects used, and if so, to what effect?

- **Information:** Particularly in a documentary film, consider how the information presented to the viewer. Does the director use music to appeal to the emotions and convince his audience? Is slow motion used? If so, when and why?

Using a viewing log can help you to keep track of what you notice while watching a film or video sequence.

Your viewing log might look like the one below, but feel free to choose different categories to fit your own purposes:

What? (sequence/ scene)	**When/Where?**	**Who?**	**Filmic devices**	**Comments/ Questions**

After viewing
Go over your viewing log again and add information or comments. Think about your overall response to the film:

What emotions does the film arouse, and through what means? Do you identify with one or more of the characters, and if so, why? Does the film try to make you take sides, or does it encourage you to draw your own conclusions? Discuss these questions with others who have seen the film and analyse the reasons for your reactions. If possible, re-examine sequences/ scenes that provoked conflicting views and discuss why you respond to them in different ways.

HOW TO WRITE A FILM REVIEW

A film review is a written text that provides information about a film. It is intended either to recommend the film in question or to discourage people from seeing it. It can also help people to form their own opinion of the film.

- Start by considering the various elements which make up a film: the characters, the setting and the plot.
- Say what the film is about, giving the title, genre, name of the director and when it was made. Among other things, you may want to include awards and the names of actors.
- Give background information on the film and the director.
- Give specific information on what the film is about and provide a short summary without giving away the ending (unless this is explicitly required). You should aim to make your audience curious and encourage them to watch the film themselves rather than give everything away.
- Finish the review with your personal opinion (on the actors' performance or the adaptation of the novel, for instance), give reasons for your opinion and say whether you would recommend it or not.
- Remember to structure your review into three main parts:
  - an introduction with a catchy first sentence,
  - a main body outlining your main points (one per paragraph),
  - a conclusion summarizing the points made.

Language help

- ▷ The film was produced/directed by ...
- ▷ It is set in / covers a period of / tells the story of ...
- ▷ The main characters are ...
- ▷ The story is rather weak/boring/unconvincing.
- ▷ The storyline is entertaining/gripping/fascinating/clever.
- ▷ I can thoroughly recommend the film.

ACKNOWLEDGEMENTS

Texts
p. 23 ISKCON Educational Services, 2004, http://hinduism.iskcon.org/lifestyle/810.htm
pp. 27 f. Matt Zoller Seitz, 'Life Lessons In A Global Marketplace', From The New York Times, September 28 © 2007 The New York Times. All rights reserved. Used by permission and protected by the Copyright Laws of the United States. The printing, copying, redistribution, or retransmission of this Content without express written permission is prohibited.
pp. 29 ff. Anand Giridharadas, 'Letter From India. Indians Adopt A Vision Under Siege In America'. From The New York Times, January 15 © 2009 The New York Times. All rights reserved. Used by permission and protected by the Copyright Laws of the United States. The printing, copying, redistribution, or retransmission of this Content without express written permission is prohibited.
p. 32 Roger Woddis: 'Godfather'. *From: One Over the 80's. Poems from the New Statesman 1982–1992* by Roger Woddis, London, Perseverance Press
pp. 36 f. Volker Müller: 'Das Ende des Indischen Callcenters'. From: Welt Online, 4 August 2009

Photos/Illustrations
Cover: Woman: Academy Films/ Cinetext; Men on bike: Brad Walker/ Getty Images
p. 5 Dmitri Mikitenko/Shutterstock
p. 12 © Jeffrey Koterba
p. 13 top Ebert/www.cartoonmovement.com; **p. 13 bottom** Cox and Forkum © 2007/www.CoxAndForkum.com
p. 14 bottom Concorde Home Ent./Cinetext
pp. 15 ff. All stills taken from the film *Outsourced:* director: John Jeffcoat, writing credits: George Wing, John Jeffcoat, produced by Tom Gorai, artists: Josh Hamilton, Ayesha Dharker and Asif Basra © Tele München Fernseh GmbH & Co. Produktionsgesellschaft
pp. 39 ff. © Holger Lipschütz